BOOK ONE

NEW ANGLES

Compiled by
John Foster

Oxford University Press

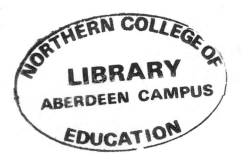
Oxford University Press, Walton Street, Oxford OX2 6DP

Oxford New York Toronto
Delhi Bombay Calcutta Madras Karachi
Petaling Jaya Singapore Hong Kong Tokyo
Nairobi Dar es Salaam Cape Town
Melbourne Auckland

and associated companies in
Berlin Ibadan

Oxford is a trade mark of Oxford University Press

© This arrangement John Foster 1987

First published 1987
Second impression 1989

ISBN 0 19 833164 9

Typeset by MS Filmsetting Limited, Frome, Somerset
Printed in Great Britain by The Alden Press, Oxford

Contents

Growing Up?

It must be, oooh,
a month or more
since they last complained
about the way I eat

or crisps I drop
on the kitchen floor

or not washing my feet

or the TV left on
when I go out

or the spoon clunking
against my teeth

or how loudly I shout

or my unmade bed,
mud on the stair,

soap left to drown
or the state of my hair...

It *must* be
a month or more.
Have they given up
in despair?

For years
they've nagged me
to grow up,
to act my age.

Can it be
that it's happened,
that I'm ready
to step out of my cage?

Wes Magee

The Unincredible Hulk-in-Law

Being the Incredible Hulk's
scrawny stepbrother ain't easy.
Sticky-fisted toddlers
pick fights with me
in misadventure playgrounds.

On beaches
seven-stone weaklings
kick sand in my eyes
vandalize my pies
and thrash me with candyfloss.

They all tell their friends
how they licked the Hulk ...
(... well not the Hulk exactly,
but an incredibly unincredible relative).

Bullied by Brownies
mugged by nuns
without a doubt
the fun's gone out
of having a TV star in the family.

Think I'll marry
Wonderwoman's asthmatic second cousin
and start a commune in Arkansas
for out-of-work, weedy
super heroes-in-law.

Roger McGough

Hairstyle

What about my hairstyle?
On my head I carry
a phosphorescent porcupine –
but it's mine it's mine
and if you don't like my head
you can drop dead.

What about my hairstyle?
On my head I bear a mane
of flaming dreadlocks
sometimes hidden by the red gold and green
but flaming all the same
with I-rie pride of Africa.
Know what I mean?

What about my hairstyle?
On my head I wear
a Mohican rainbow
that makes me glow.
I know some eyebrows go
up in despair
but it's my hair it's my hair.

What about my hairstyle?
On my head I show a crown
Of incandescent candy floss.
Who cares if some people frown
and say, 'Young people are lost'.
At least me Mum doesn't get on me back;
she says, 'I suppose you're only young once'.

What about my hairstyle?
On my head I have whispers
of braided beads.
Me Mum says she wouldn't have the patience –
but these beads are in no hurry
I tell them my needs
they listen to the song inside of me.

John Agard

Hundreds and Thousands

Under the hair-drier,
Under the hair,

The head of my sister
Is dreaming of where

She sits by the sea-shore
On somebody's yacht,

Drinking and thinking
And dreaming of what

She'll buy with her hundreds
And thousands of dollars,

Like ten silver tom-cats
With golden flea-collars

To yawn round the lawn
Of her garden in France

Where she lies by the pool
As the blue ripples dance,

And millions of brilliant
People dive in,

All loaded with money
And honey and gin,

All wonderfully funny
With witty remarks

As the sun in the water
Makes shivering sparks

And there by the pool
She lies browning and basking as

All of the people cry,
'Thank you for asking us!'

That's what I read
In her dopey sea-stare

Under the hair-drier,
Under the hair.

Gloria's
shampoo
Shampoo &
set
Back combing
Tint's.
Blue, green,
yellow, pink
Trims
styling

She wakes from her dreaming
Of making a mint

And – *would you believe it?* –
She's UTTERLY SKINT!

She's stealing all *my*
Pocket money from *me*!

'I'm off to the Disco –
Need 20 more p!'

> *Kit Wright*

I'm the Big Sleeper

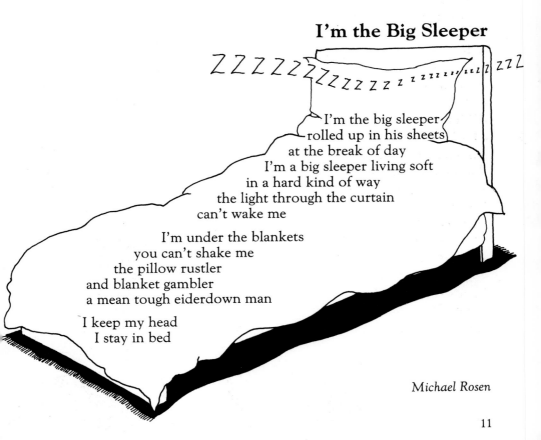

ZZZZZZZZZZ Z Z Z Z Z Z Z Z Z Z Z Z ZZZ

I'm the big sleeper
rolled up in his sheets
at the break of day
I'm a big sleeper living soft
in a hard kind of way
the light through the curtain
can't wake me

I'm under the blankets
you can't shake me
the pillow rustler
and blanket gambler
a mean tough eiderdown man

I keep my head
I stay in bed

> *Michael Rosen*

11

You'll See

They all talked about growing into,
Growing into, growing into.
They said: You will grow into it.

– But it isn't mine,
And it's not for me.
– You will grow into it,
You'll see!

– But it hangs down below my knee,
It is too long for me.
– Oh it will fit you soon,
It will fit you splendidly.

– But I will sulk, and I will say
It is too long, it is no use,
No! I will sulk, and struggle,
And refuse!

– You will grow into it,
And love it,
And besides, we decided
You should have it.

NO! – But wait –
Wait a moment ... Do I see
It growing shorter at the knee?
Is it shrinking gradually?
Is it getting shorter?
Is it getting tighter?
Not loose and straggly,
Not long and baggy,
But neater and brighter,
Comfortable?

Oh now I *do* like it,
Oh now I'll go to the mirror and see
How wonderful it looks on me,
Yes – there – it's ideal!
Yes, it's appeal
Will be universal,
And now I curse all
Those impulses which muttered 'Refuse!'
It's really beautiful after all,
I'll wear it today, next week, next year
– No one is going to interfere,
I'll wear it as long as I choose.

And then, much later, when it wears
And it's ready for dumping under the stairs
When it doesn't actually really fit me
Any longer, then *I'll* pass it down,
I'll give it to someone else
When it doesn't fit me,
And then they'll have it,
They'll *have* to have it,
They'll have to love it,
They'll see, they'll see.

They'll have to grow into it like me.

Alan Brownjohn

Beatings

My father beats me up
Just like his father did
And grandad he was beaten
by greatgrandad as a kid

From generation to generation
A poisoned apple passed along
Domestic daily cruelty
No one thinking it was wrong.

And it was:

Not the cursing and the bruising
The frustration and the fear
A normal child can cope with that
It grows easier by the year

But the ignorance, believing
That the child is somehow owned
Property paid for
Violence condoned.

Roger McGough

14

Home is where you hang your hat
And can't get a break
Home is what you ought to want
But can't really make

Home is where you're always wrong
Too fat or too thin
Home's an endless argument
You never can win

Home is a test you always fail
Emotions you have to fake
Where everybody does his thing
For somebody else's sake

Home is where love's old sweet song
Just won't set you free
Home is where you're not the way
They want you to be

Home sweet home will haunt your dreams
Wherever you go
Home is what there's no place like
But didn't you know
Home is where the heartache
Really started

Fran Landesman

Street Boy

Just you look at me, man,
Stompin' down the street
My crombie stuffed with biceps
My boots is filled with feet.

Just you hark to me, man,
When they call us out
My head is full of silence
My mouth is full of shout.

Just you watch me move, man,
Steady like a clock
My heart is spaced on blue beat
My soul is stoned on rock.

Just you read my name, man,
Writ for all to see
The walls is red with stories
The streets is filled with me.

Gareth Owen

Earrings

I'm lying in her used bath water,
thinking we ought to get a bucket,
bale it over the parched roses.

She's perched on the toilet seat
eating an Eccles cake.

Lukewarm ripples lap my navel.
I drink hot coffee –
she's made it too strong.

She reads the sheet
the hairdresser gave her

rotates the small gold studs
– three times forward, three times back –
dabs her ears with surgical spirit.

Stares at herself in the mirror.
'My ears aren't level.

Shall I scrub your back?'

Patricia Pogson

Mother of the Groom

What she remembers
Is his glistening back
In the bath, his small boots
In the ring of boots at her feet.

Hands in her voided lap,
She hears a daughter welcomed.
It's as if he kicked when lifted
And slipped her soapy hold.

Once soap would ease off
The wedding ring
That's bedded forever now
In her clapping hand.

Seamus Heaney

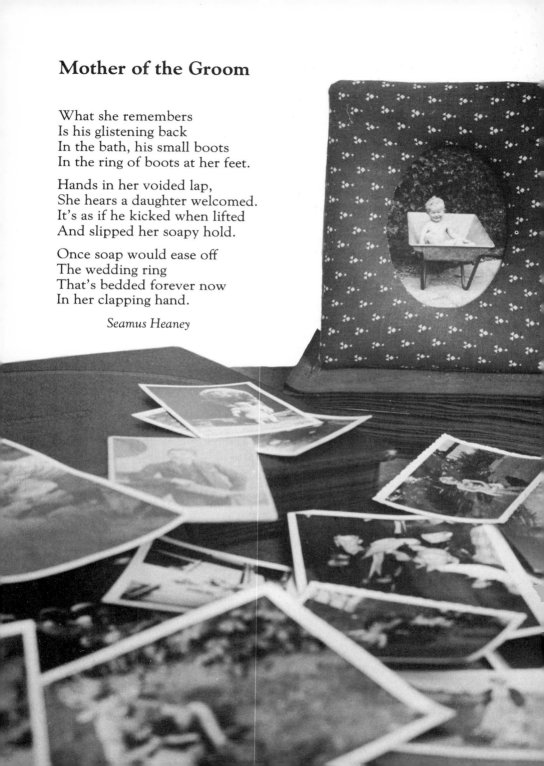

Transformations

'Well, well, we've grown!'
My uncle,
stubble-chinned,
nails blackened by
a lifetime in the fields
of furrowed Lincolnshire.
Hair roughly stacked
on wind-pocked face;
few words, though
'How you've grown!'
served well enough to raise
a childish moan.

Some ten years on,
the stubble thinned,
knuckles deeper-ploughed
with black on brown.
Words, much the same;
stoop, lower; face,
furrowed. And ten years on
at least I have the grace
on hearing how I've grown
to hold my tongue
and still the childish moan.

Another dozen years;
my uncle, teeth and stubble gone
lies pale behind his boyish fears.
No words, no nod.
The old man dreams alone
knowing now, perhaps,
his growing's done;
whilst I,
with children of my own
must turn to them
and wonder how
and when
to still their childish song.

Judith Nicholls

Christmas Thank You's

Dear Auntie

Oh what a nice jumper
I've always adored powder blue
and fancy you thinking of
orange and pink
for the stripes
how clever of you!

Dear Cousin

What socks!
and the same sort you wear
so you must be
the last word in style
and I'm certain you're right that the
luminous green
will make me stand out a mile.

Dear Gran

Many thanks for the hankies
Now I really can't wait for the fun
and the daisies embroidered
in red round the 'M'
for Michael
how
thoughtful of you!

Dear Uncle

The soap is
terrific
So
useful
and such a kind thought and
how did you guess that
I'd just used the last of
the soap that last Christmas brought.

Dear Sister

I quite understand your concern
It's a risk sending jam in the post
But I think I've pulled out
all the big bits
of glass
so it won't taste too sharp
spread on toast.

Dear Grandad
Don't fret
I'm delighted
So _don't_ think your gift will
offend
I'm not at all hurt
that you gave up this year
and just sent me
a fiver
to spend.

Mick Gowar

Film Star

He was a rich pin-up boy – Mercedes, plane, etc.
His smile, like the winter sun, was bright,
But didn't warm you. One side of his face
Was handsome – the side that caught the light
   In front of the cameras.

And all the girls adored him.

His days were a whirlwind of wonders: he fell off
Mountains, jumped out of the sky, fought
With twenty at a time, went down with his ship
Smiling – it was all the bravest sport –
   In front of the cameras.

And all the girls adored him.

But was the smile his own? Yes, but never
The danger. That burning driver in the prairie race
Was another man. Where was the rich pin-up boy then?
Reading his newspaper in a safer place –
   Behind the cameras.

And all the girls adored him.

Weeks later, on his way to the studio, he crashed
His Mercedes, cut his face (the handsome side). O cruel blow!
Fifteen days he lay on his back, a little boy
Frightened of the dark, crying for mother. He wouldn't go
   In front of the cameras.

And all the girls forgot him.

        Ian Serraillier

Elvis: The Poem

Bounty hunter
from my far West
he gyrated
into TV town
and holed up at
Heartbreak Hotel;
the guitar-slinger
with a lip sneer
for whom madams
and molls grew moist
at a wriggle of
his little finger.

Eds and Ellas frowned;
others thumped Bibles
as he cleaned up in
Nashville's saloons
where no one rolled
a hip faster.
On every wall
his name and mug-shot
– the most wanted man,
before fast food,
ice-cream soddened him:
tears on Boot Hill.

Best remember
the lanky kid
casual against a
gas pump in Memphis
while, behind him, the
pick-up truck idles.
On its front seat
an old strum-box
warming in the day,
and climbing sky-high
the sun's gold disc
not yet in his sights.

Wes Magee

Guitarman

I play my Guild guitar like a sub-machine gun,
spraying out music while these fingers make their runs
across the hopscotch of a fretboard
in steps and turns,
a sword of a plectrum strokes the strings
and booming from the box's crater
a lava of sound oozes out.

I'm a guitarman,
I'm a magnetic island
which the strobe lights cling to.
And all I do is let loose from silence
a running stampede of notes
as my hair swings
with its strands of wire.
I feel tense in a punishing duel
between myself and the audience.
I lift my guitar like a railway signal,
unmoved; except my tremulous fingers,
always aiming steady as I fire.

Gordon Phillips

On the Disco Floor

Laser beams
   make dreams
   of my head
Smoke lights
   ferriswheel
   down my eyes
and I feel
   the night
   is a horse
we're riding
   to nowhere
But if the feeling
   is all right
   with you
   it's all right
   with me
   So hold tight
   hold the mane
   of midnight
and kiss me again

John Agard

You Make Me So Nervous

You make me so nervous
You make me so tense
I snap and I stammer
It doesn't make sense

You make me so nervous
I talk much too fast
And when we're both happy
I'm scared it won't last

The pleasure you give me at moments
Is more than my pen can express
But why do you give me the feeling
That I'm such a terrible mess

When you're in a bad mood
You make me so sad
I simply can't bear it
You're driving me mad

But all of my worries
Dissolve when we touch
You make me so nervous
I love you so much

Fran Landesman

Riddle-Me-Ree

My first is in life (not contained within heart)
My second's in whole but never in part.
My third's in forever, but also in vain.
My last's in ending, why not in pain?

¿ɹǝʍsuɐ ǝɥʇ ǝʌoʃ sı

Liz Lochhead

Lost Love Poem

One day they'll manufacture eggs,
The formula for snowflakes will be clear
And love explained – that's not the day
I think about, the day I marked on my calendar.

Because they appreciate their legs,
Simple creatures will career
Through boundless grass. One day, the day
I think about, the day I marked on my calendar.

In the classroom the boy with ragged fingernails
Flicks a note to the girl whose hair solidifies
All the light there is. The note says:
Some day, when I'm grown up, some day –
It falls between the floorboards. . . .

Adrian Mitchell

27

Good-Night

A latch lifting, an edged den of light
Opens across the yard. Out of the low door
They stoop into the honeyed corridor,
Then walk straight through the wall of the dark.

A puddle, cobble-stones, jambs and doorstep
Are set steady in a block of brightness.
Till she strides in again beyond her shadows
And cancels everything behind her.

Seamus Heaney

A Girl's Song

Early one morning
As I went out walking
I saw the young sailor
Go fresh through the fields.
His eye was as blue as
The sky up above us
And clean was his skin
As the colour of shells.

O where are you going,
Young sailor, so early?
And may I come with you
A step as you go?
He looked with his eye
And I saw the deep sea-tombs,
He opened his mouth
And I heard the sea roar.

And limp on his head
Lay his hair green as sea-grass
And scrubbed were his bones
By the inching of sand.
The long tides enfolded
The lines of his body
And slow corals grow
At the stretch of his hand.

I look from my window
In the first light of morning
And I look from my door
At the dark of the day,
But all that I see are
The fields flat and empty
And the black road run down
To Cardigan town.

Leslie Norris

The Thickness of Ice

At first we will meet as friends
(Though secretly I'll be hoping
We'll become much more
And hoping that you're hoping that too).

At first we'll be like skaters
Testing the thickness of ice
(With each meeting
We'll skate nearer the centre of the lake).

Later we will become less anxious to impress,
Less eager than the skater going for gold,
(The triple jumps and spins
Will become an old routine:
We will be content with simple movements).

Later we will not notice the steady thaw,
The creeping cracks will be ignored,
(And one day when the ice gives way
We will scramble to save ourselves
And not each other).

Last of all we'll meet as acquaintances
(Though secretly we will be enemies,
Hurt by missing out on a medal,
Jealous of new partners).

Last of all we'll be like children
Having learnt the thinness of ice,
(Though secretly, perhaps, we may be hoping
To break the ice between us
And maybe meet again as friends).

Liz Loxley

There is Only One Story

There is only one story:
he loved her,
then stopped loving her,
while she did not
stop loving him.

There is only one story:
she loved him,
then stopped loving him,
while he did not
stop loving her.

The truth is simple:
you do not die
from love.
You only wish
you did.

Erica Jong

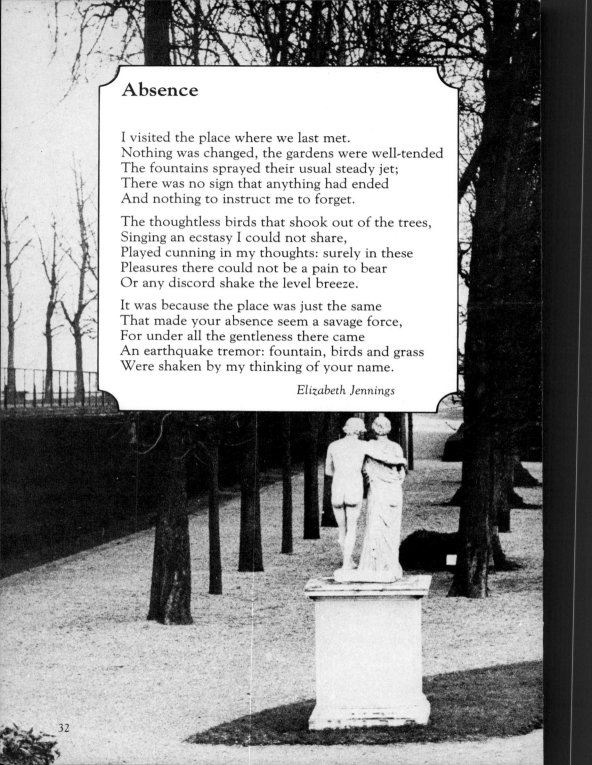

Absence

I visited the place where we last met.
Nothing was changed, the gardens were well-tended
The fountains sprayed their usual steady jet;
There was no sign that anything had ended
And nothing to instruct me to forget.

The thoughtless birds that shook out of the trees,
Singing an ecstasy I could not share,
Played cunning in my thoughts: surely in these
Pleasures there could not be a pain to bear
Or any discord shake the level breeze.

It was because the place was just the same
That made your absence seem a savage force,
For under all the gentleness there came
An earthquake tremor: fountain, birds and grass
Were shaken by my thinking of your name.

Elizabeth Jennings

Sometimes it Happens

And sometimes it happens that you are friends and then
You are not friends,
And friendship has passed.
And whole days are lost and among them
A fountain empties itself.

And sometimes it happens that you are loved and then
You are not loved,
And love is past.
And whole days are lost and among them
A fountain empties itself into the grass.

And sometimes you want to speak to her and then
You do not want to speak,
Then the opportunity has passed.
Your dreams flare up, they suddenly vanish.

And also it happens that there is nowhere to go and then
There is somewhere to go,
Then you have bypassed.
And the years flare up and are gone,
Quicker than a minute.

So you have nothing.
You wonder if these things matter and then
As soon as you begin to wonder if these things matter
They cease to matter,
And caring is past.
And a fountain empties itself into the grass.

Brian Patten

Rain

when the rain is falling in long columns

we are inclined to forget what a miracle it is.

George Macbeth

Watch Your Step, I'm Drenched

In Manchester there are a thousand puddles.
Bus-queue puddles poised on slanting paving stones,
Railway puddles slouching outside stations,
Cinema puddles in ambush at the exits,
Zebra-crossing puddles in dips of the dark stripes –
They lurk in the murk
Of the north-western evening
For the sake of their notorious joke,
Their only joke – to soak
The tights or trousers of the citizens.
Each splash and consequent curse is echoed by
One thousand dark Mancunian puddle chuckles.

In Manchester there lives the King of Puddles,
Master of Miniature Muck Lakes,
The Shah of Slosh, Splendifero of Splash,
Prince, Pasha and Pope of Puddledom.
Where? Somewhere. The rain-headed ruler
Lies doggo, incognito,
Disguised as an average, accidental mini-pool.
He is scared as any other emperor,
For one night, all his soiled and soggy victims
Might storm his streets, assassination in their minds,
A thousand rolls of blotting paper in their hands,
And drink his shadowed, one-joke life away.

Adrian Mitchell

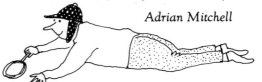

35

The Long Walk

The sun feels hot as opening an oven door.

As I bend beneath my rucksack
And slog up the slope
Drops of sweat run down my nose
And moisten the moor.
No wonder I said to the rabbit we passed
That stood and watched and didn't scare,
'You must be thinking I'm a fool
To be doing this'.

But if the petrol evaporated,
The power stations switched off,
The railway was taken to pieces
And the road broke,
It wouldn't matter to us
And that's why we're singing.

Stanley Cook

Dog Exercising Man

From the way
    they look at
        each other
it is clear
    that the man
        and the dog
are friends but
    in this park
        this morning
man does not
    exercise
        dog. On the
contrary:
    in tracksuit
        and plimsolls
the man is
    jogging eggs
        and bacon
away round
    the railings
        while the dog
is trotting
    doggedly
        as it must
along a
    concentric
        shorter track
within ear-
    shot doubtless
        wondering
what there is
    to be fetched
        and hoping
that man will
    soon mark his
        territory.

Keith Bosley

Beginner's Luck

Well, he had his fibreglass rod
With a fixed spool reel
And monafilament line,
The kind you read about
In the angling magazines
Or stand daydreaming over
In the angling shop
Till the man there wants to know
What it is, if anything,
You're going to buy;

And while he studied
His box of assorted flies
And weights for his float
Of graded size
The brown, red-speckled fish
Lay at anchor
In the shadows of the stream.

And while he watched the eddies
And looked for a likely spot
With overhanging boughs
From where he could ambush
The unsuspecting fish,
I with my bamboo cane
With a worm on a pin
At the end of a piece of string
Was hauling them in.

Stanley Cook

Live Baiting

It isn't nice, the way I fish:
Kidnapping roach from quiet ponds,
And spitting them on hooks
For pike to eat.
They swim, you could say, freely; live bait,
Unconstrained by locks,
But tethered by lip or fin, their bonds
Almost invisible, the barbs buried in flesh.

Each cast gives them the chance
To die. Scalded by air
They plummet thirty yards upstream,
Bombing the shallows, targets
That swim into the sights
Of what will kill them.
Pike aren't interested in playing at war,
They meet their partners in an older dance.

The one I caught today wore
Like a brooch a hook of mine, lost
When the line broke months ago.
I found it rooted
In her throat. When I gutted
Her, eggs lined her belly like orange sago.
Pain has no memory, grief stays in the past.
It isn't true. I can't fish this way any more.

Philip Oakes

The Salmon Fisher to the Salmon

The ridged lip set upstream, you flail
Inland again, your exile in the sea
Unconditionally cancelled by the pull
    Of your home water's gravity.

And I stand in the centre, casting.
The river cramming under me reflects
Slung gaff and net and a white wrist flicking
    Flies well-dressed with tint and fleck.

Walton thought garden worms, perfumed
By oil crushed from dark ivy berries
The lure that took you best, but here you come
    To grief through hunger in your eyes.

Ripples arrowing beyond me,
The current strumming water up my leg,
Involved in water's choreography
    I go, like you, by gleam and drag

And will strike when you strike, to kill.
We're both annihilated on the fly.
You can't resist a gullet full of steel.
    I will turn home fish-smelling, scaly.

Seamus Heaney

The Perch Pool

Somewhere there
In the oval bowl
That lies between the new
Precinct for pedestrians
And the bare, glassy cliff
Of the Commercial Union
Used to be grandpa's pool.
And in the hollow of green banks,
Buffed to a shine by steely skies,
The cool,
Mysterious water ringed by reeds
Still quietly lies.

One tiny gravel beach
Dips beneath surface circles
Where the minnows rise
Over the reach of water
Where they say the pit-shaft slides
To unimaginable, legendary depths
In which the pike-god hides.

There grandpa used to kneel by reeds
And in the wet heaven of the water-weeds
The smooth-skinned frog
With breast stroke flash of slender legs
Squeezed the cool power of water in its wake,
Thrust silently without a splash,
And on its back
Arrowed the surface with a young one's head.

Beside the dusty flower-bed
Grandpa sat on the bench;
His legs were tired,
So he relaxed and stared
Into the concrete slabbing of his pool.
The child fingered the old man's face –
'Tell me about the frogs,' he said,
Wriggling alongside grandpa on the seat.

Grandpa lifted his jacket sleeve and sniffed.
'Smell that,' he said,
'That shower of rain on tweed' –
'The what? The frogs, yes, hid in the weed,
And then they used to race,
Webbing their way in bubble lace
Across the pool
With that easy, slack
Flash of their feet,
And young ones riding piggy-back.'

And then he stopped,
The boy's head cupped
In his lumpy fingers.
The child knew better than interrupt,
For grandpa's gaze
Was fixed, through the distant trees and cars
On the sudden splash and blaze
Of fat perch with their tiger bars.

Gregory Harrison

Going

Crossing alone
the dark glassy surface
of the lake among the trees
where no one else is;
I drift, halfway
between the rotting boathouse
and the hidden landing-stage
sinking in the sedge
that shifts and whispers
although there is no breeze.
A pale heron stands
still, on one leg, to watch
my slow ragged row
in the heavy boat I borrow
each time I'm here:
my hollow *thuds* and splashes sink
deep into the black
woods that go up steep
and topple into sky –
no sound of me comes back.
Alone, I hardly spoil
this motionless expanse
at all; as if oil
were what I slid across
my slow progressions close
up behind me,
instantaneous.
Where I am now,
now is a moment ago,
a memory I may
forget, myself, one day . . .

Between what comes and goes
or stays, or moves
there is an edge that is
always, here and now,
narrower than a knife,
cutting into my life,
and making it my own:
I feel the future flow
into me, and through
and instantly renew,
as underneath the prow,
clear, continuous,
the waters stay, but go,
still, but slipping past,
as they move, or I move,
going, slow or fast,
reflecting sky and sedge,
depth, below, above,
and in between them, I,
on my way, here and now,
in an eternity,
out, always, on time's edge.

Brian Lee

Boats for Hire

Drifting through fallen
floating leaves, trailing its oars

like two broken wings, our rowing boat
nudged the muddy bank, startling a swan and his mate

We watched them rise,
followed their climb away from us,

and wished for them
a quiet lake, where only

their own reflections glide
between them on the water.

And you cannot pay
to row across it.

Tony Flynn

The Swimmer

He clings to the water, cleaves
It to him then kicks and shoves
The wet around him, heaves
His chest and shoulders, moves
Into an old dimension.
His instincts take over,
He achieves suspension
In a space full of forever,
A place familiar as a stone's splash
Into a running river
Or a wave's cautious crash
On the edge
Of a sunset-sucking ocean.

Now he's in another age,
Blows bubbles underwater
And watches the air
Take a shine to itself, so clear
It seems to clean the atmosphere.
He shakes himself, lashes out
And presses on
Now that the game's afoot.
He swims, he's having fun
Fancying himself, without a fin,
As a boy becoming dolphin;
Seeing himself take first place
In an inhuman race.
Still, that's a myth,
An aspect of the truth
That hardly touches this liquid moment
That finds him in his element.

Alan Bold

Slow Guitar

Bring me now where the warm wind
blows, where the grasses
sigh, where the sweet
tongued blossom flowers

where the showers
fan soft like a fisherman's
net through the sweet-
ened air

Bring me now where the workers
rest, where the cotton drifts,
where the rivers are
and the minstrel sits

on the logwood stump
with the dreams of his slow guitar.

Edward Kamau Brathwaite

Heatwave

Heat over all; not a lark can rise
Into the arching sun;
The moor like a lion sleeping lies –
Rough mane on burning stone.
Not a harebell shakes; the wild blue flags
Of wind are folded up.
Here on the hill the air is still
As water in a cup.

Phoebe Hesketh

The Silence Lesson

A butterfly
clapped its wings
shut:
    the cry went up
    ssh!

A startled bird
knocked a feather
against a ray of light:
    the cry went up
    ssh!

So the elephant on its drum
so man on his earth
learned to walk
    without making
    a sound.

Trees sprang up
dumb above the fields
their hair
    on
    end.

Keith Bosley
(after *Tymoteusz Karpowicz*)

Kept Home

I look out of my high-up window.
I see chimney tops, fences, scattered trees,
in this sunny summer-Saturday.

Our white cat strolls
across the neighbour's newly cut grass.
Birds are noisy.
A wind teases branches
and gardens of flowers.

I can't see far on my left.
The silver birch spreads
elegant branches before me,
fluttering its leaves like
a lady's shiny frills in sunlight.

Girls and boys play football,
smaller ones are swinging,
in the playground
and view of the church ...

Out and out, past all streets
and housetops and trees, the sky
touches our Lookfar Hill,
with a smoky white light surrounding.

When holidays come, any day now,
and I'm well, fit again,
I shall clamber up
Lookfar's hillside tracks...

An iron bird roars ...
Aeroplane breaks the clouds.
It sails in open space.
Who are on board?
Who? I wonder ...

Travelling or staying at home,
people wait to get somewhere –
wait for something to happen,
something to end, begin or develop ...

Sunlight floods my room suddenly.
Shadows move on one wall
like reflections
of a busy open flame.

Sounds of motor cars get louder.
Every day our world is its own
moving picture show ...
What crazy new character can I add? ...

James Berry

Snapshots

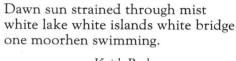

Dawn sun strained through mist
white lake white islands white bridge
one moorhen swimming.

Keith Bosley

The gutter is edged with diamonds
  the birds are drinking them

Pierre Reverdy

Did you see the swan
fly over the street?

Your black hair has gone
grey: have you noticed
your life is passing?

Votyak folk poem

Laughing at the clouds the lightning, warrior
  unwearied in the fight
or watchman asleep at night
  who cocks an eye, then shuts it.

Judah A L-Harizi

The sun fights its way to bed – in the dusk
    its disc stains the snow red:
an old scar that long since bled
    and an old wound unclotted.

Alun Llwyd

She plays: O the heart's alarm as the lute
    delights with its wild charm –
a child on its mother's arm
    crying to her song's rhythm.

Judah A L-Harizi

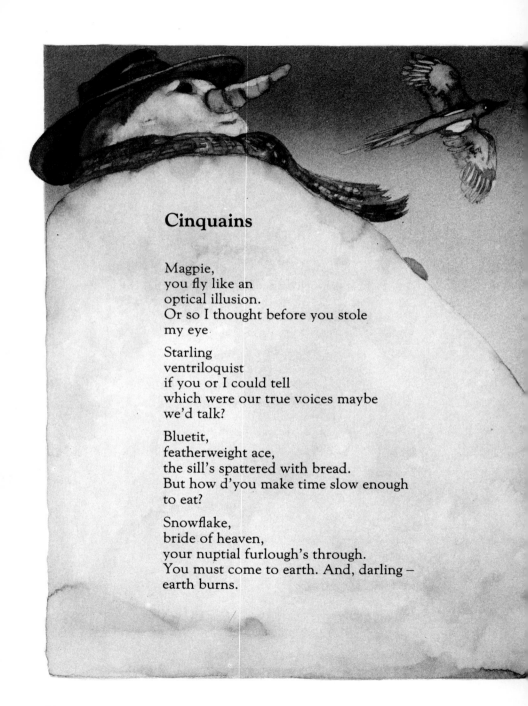

Cinquains

Magpie,
you fly like an
optical illusion.
Or so I thought before you stole
my eye.

Starling
ventriloquist
if you or I could tell
which were our true voices maybe
we'd talk?

Bluetit,
featherweight ace,
the sill's spattered with bread.
But how d'you make time slow enough
to eat?

Snowflake,
bride of heaven,
your nuptial furlough's through.
You must come to earth. And, darling –
earth burns.

Snowman,
pudgy scarecrow,
you look to the cold moon.
But can that aimless bitch transfix
the sun?

Swansdown,
wild white roses
on the river's green bough,
in what sad driftwood will your skiffs
crumple?

Scarlet
geranium
the felt pens of your buds
are busting to splash summer on
my sill.

Allow
the barnacle
its half inch, the groundsel
its nick between stones. Let life
live life.

Geoffrey Holloway

One Way of Flying

As in a dream, you need
no machine, or shrieking jet –
no take-off or landing
need bother you at all.

You just push off from
nothing, into the dark rim
of outer space, wearing only
an eagle cap, boots, jumpsuit.

And all you need is wings of
fantasy like a butterfly bat's
and a sailship's rigging
on which to brace your feet.

Your arms, flung wide, as in sleep –
knees bent for the slalom of stars –
hands grip the membrane of a dream –
hang-glider of the haunted airs.

James Kirkup

Gymnast

On rings
of air
and ropes
of muscle
swings
a body
tense
as steel
and yet
so warm –

as hard
as rock
and yet
so fluent –

water moves
like this
controlled
yet free –

with joy
and pain
with care
and with
abandon
to the cross
of space
where he
must hang
by bleeding hands

James Kirkup

Hero

'Of course I took the drugs. Look son,
there's no fairplay, no gentlemen,
no amateurs – just winning.
No one runs for fun – well, not beyond
the schoolboy stuff – eleven or twelve years old.
I'd been a pro. for years;
my job – to get that Gold.

Mind you, we English are an odd lot
like to believe we love the slob that fails,
the gentlemanly third; so any gap-toothed yob who gets the glory
also gets some gentlemanly trait: helps cripples get across
the street, nice to small animals. You know the kind of thing,
it helps the public feel it's
all legit; that sportsmanship is real and that
it's all clean fun –
the strongest, bravest, fittest
best man won.

Yeah, Steroids ... Who do *you* think? ... Oh, don't be wet –
My coach, of course, he used to get them
through this vet ... The side effects? Well, not so bad
as these things go – for eighteen months or so
I didn't have much use for girls. But, by then I was training
for the Big One – got to keep the body pure,
not waste an ounce of effort.'

He gives a great guffaw –
a chain of spittal
rattles down the front of
his pyjama jacket.
He wipes his mouth;
his eyes don't laugh at all.

'... Do it again? Of course I would –
I'd cheat, I'd box, I'd spike, I'd pay the devil's price
to be that good again
for just one day. You see, at twenty-three
I peaked – got all I ever wanted:
all anyone would ever want from me.
After the race this interviewer told me
50 million people's hopes and dreams had been
fulfilled – A Gold!
How many ever get that chance – I did.
Would you say No to that?
Of course not.

Damn, the bell. You'd better go, they're pretty strict.
Yeah, leave the flowers there – on the top,
the nurse'll get some water and a vase.'

Mick Gowar

Viv

Like the sun rising and setting
Like the thunderous roar of a bull rhino
Like the sleek, quick grace of a gazelle,
The player springs into the eye
And lights the world with fires
Of a million dreams, a million aspirations.
The batsman-hero climbs the skies,
Strikes the earth-ball for six
And the landscape rolls with the ecstasy of the magic play.

Through the covers, the warrior thrusts a majestic cut
Lighting the day with runs
As bodies reel and tumble,
Hands clap, eyes water
And hearts move inside out.

The volcano erupts!
Blows the game apart.

Faustin Charles

Can't Be Bothered to Think of a Title

When they make slouching in the chair
an Olympic sport
I'll be there.

When they give out a cup
for refusing to get up
I'll win it every year.

When they hand out the gold
for sitting by the fire
I'll leave the others in the cold.

And when I'm asked to sign my name
in the Apathetic Hall of Fame
I won't go.

Ian McMillan

Cup-Final

T. O'Day

W. E. March   T. O. G. Lory

J. Usty   O. Uwait   N. See

G. O'Dow
A. Day   W. Ewill   N. Infa   H. I. Story

Young   N. Fast   M. O'Reskill   I. T. Sreally
W. Egot

A. L. L. Sewnup   W. E. Rethel   A. D. S. Whollrun

A. Round   W. Embley

W. I. Thecup

Roger McGough

Attending a Football Match

It sneaked past watchful attendants,
warned to be on the look-out for It
among the male together-noise.
White faces on dark clothes
cohered, shading the terracing
to the anonymous crouch of a crowd.

The ninepin players trotted in.
Kinetic muscles moved in play,
and Matt, John, Jock and Wullie
bounced on their excitement's cheers.

But as the ball began to score
goals spent in a stretched net,
It wedged Itself between the roars
of the single-backed, two-minded thing,
for *game*, insinuated *name*,
a syllableless, faceless feeling
of nothing words identified.

Then suddenly It broke loose –
bottles hit fists and screams.
Police tore the crowd apart
to get It. It eluded them.

From spectators crushed by shock,
a swearing vanful of louts,
the cut-up quiet in hospitals,
no real evidence could be taken.
Charges were, of course preferred –
disorderly conduct, obstructing the police –
but no one found out what It was
or whose It is, or where It came from.

Maurice Lindsay

Whippet

Barbed head
pointed with purpose.

Chest clenched
stringing the starving ribs.

A caricature:
pinching waist, thighs bursting.

It yawns:

jaw pulls back on ratchets
to crack its thin wedge face;

the coiled muscle trap springs
shut to snap the air.

Andrew Hall

Hundredsandthousands

The sound of hounds
on red sand thundering

Hundreds and thousands
of mouths glistening

The blood quickening
Thunder and lightning

The hunted in dread
of the hundreds running

The sound of thunder
A white moon reddening

Thousands of mad hounds
on red sand marauding

Thundering onwards
in hundreds and thundreds

Thundreds and thundreds
Thundering   Thundering.

Roger McGough

Foxhunt

Two days after Xmas, near noon, as I listen
The hounds behind the hill
Are changing ground, a cloud of excitements,
Their voices like rusty, reluctant
Rolling stock being shunted. The hunt
Has tripped over a fox
At the threshold of the village. A crow in the fir
Is inspecting his nesting site, and he expostulates
At the indecent din. A blackbird
Starts up its cat-alarm. The grey-cloud mugginess
Of the year in its pit trying to muster
Enough energy to start opening again
Roars distantly. Everything sodden. The fox
Is flying, taking his first lesson
From the idiot pack-noise, the puppyish whine-yelps
Curling up like hounds' tails, and the gruff military barkers:
A machine with only two products:

Dog-shit and dead foxes. Lorry engines
As usual modulating on the main street hill
Complicate the air, and the fox runs in a suburb
Of indifferent civilised noises. Now the yelpings
Enrich their brocade, thickening closer
In the maze of wind-currents. The orchards
And the hedges stand in coma. The pastures
Have got off so far lightly, are firm, cattle
Still nose hopefully, as if spring might be here
Missing out winter. Big lambs
Are organising their gangs in gateways. The fox
Hangs his silver tongue in the world of noise
Over his spattering paws. Will he run
Till his muscles suddenly turn to iron,
Till blood froths his mouth as his lungs tatter,
Till his feet are raw blood-sticks and his tail
Trails thin as a rat's? Or will he
Make a mistake, jump the wrong way, jump right
Into the hound's mouth? As I write this down
He runs still fresh, with all his chances before him.

Ted Hughes

The Fox

A fox among the shadows of the town,
Should I surrender to the arms of man?
  On the blank icehills lies in wait
  The fighting cold who has thrown down
  His challenge. I'll not imitate
  The feline compromise. I scan
  With warring eyes the servile fate
Of animals who joined the heated town.

Lean-hearted lions in the concrete zoo
Grow bellies, tendons slacken in pale hide,
  Their breath slows to a dying pace.
  Their keepers love them? Tell me who
  Would cage his love in such a place,
  Where only fish are satisfied?
  The keeper has a huntsman's face.
His grasping love would kill me in the zoo.

A scavenger throughout the snowing wind
I peel the sweet bark from the frozen tree
  Or trap the bird with springing jaws.
  The sun retreats out of my mind.
  How could I give this waking pause
  When death's my sleeping company?
  Mad empty, licking at my sores,
I howl this bitter and unloving wind.

Furious in the savage winter day
The crimson riders hounded me from birth
   Through landscapes built of thorn and stone.
   Though I must be their sudden prey,
   Torn to my terror's skeleton,
   Or go to the forgotten earth;
   I will have hunted too, alone,
I will have wandered in my handsome day.

Four seasons wrestle me, I throw them all
And live to tumble with another year
   In love or battle. I'll not fly
   From mindless elements and fall
   A victim to the keeper's lie.
   The field is mine; but still I fear
   Strong death, my watching enemy,
Though seasons pass and I survive them all.

Adrian Mitchell

Pigeons

They paddle with staccato feet
In powder-pools of sunlight,
Small blue busybodies
Strutting like fat gentlemen
With hands clasped
Under their swallowtail coats;
And, as they stump about,
Their heads like tiny hammers
Tap at imaginary nails
In non-existent walls.
Elusive ghosts of sunshine
Slither down the green gloss
Of their necks an instant, and are gone.

Summer hangs drugged from sky to earth
In limpid fathoms of silence:
Only warm dark dimples of sound
Slide like slow bubbles
From the contented throats.

Raise a casual hand –
With one quick gust
They fountain into air.

Richard Kell

Kingfisher

Brown as nettle-beer, the stream
Shadow-freckled, specked with sun,
Slides between the trees.

Not a ripple breaks in foam;
Only the frilled hedge-parsley falls
White upon the ground.
No insect drills the air; no sound
Rustles among the reeds.
Bird and leaf and thought are still
When shot from the blue, a kingfisher
Flashes between the ferns –
Jewelled torpedo sparkling by
Under the bridge and gone –
Yet bright as a bead behind the eye,
The image blazes on.

Phoebe Hesketh

Town Owl

On eves of cold, when slow coal fires,
rooted in basements, burn and branch,
brushing with smoke the city air;

When quartered moons pale in the sky,
and neons glow along the dark
like deadly nightshade on a briar;

Above the muffled traffic then
I hear the owl, and at his note
I shudder in my private chair.

For like an augur he has come
to roost among our crumbling walls,
his blooded talons sheathed in fur.

Some secret lure of time it seems
has called him from his country wastes
to hunt a newer wasteland here.

And where the candelabra swung,
bright with the dancers' thousand eyes,
now his black, hooded pupils stare,

And where the silk-shoed lovers ran
with dust of diamonds in their hair,
he opens now his silent wing,

And, like a stroke of doom, drops down,
and swoops across the empty hall,
and plucks a quick mouse off the stair . . .

Laurie Lee

Kestrel

He lay on his breast against the house wall
The brass rings of his eyes still polished.
He must have arrowed full-tilt
Into the first floor windowglass
Making just one mistake
About space.

Handsomely banded sweeping wings,
Half-folded, hunched his shoulders
Like the pinions of a tabby angel.
His face narrowed wisely
To the small beak like a single horn
Delicately designed to hinge apart
And rend flesh.

After a week he's nothing.
Only his hard legs are fierce,
Stretching out talons
Hollow, flexible, smooth,
The colour of polished lava.

He lies on his back now, wings fallen apart,
Head like a wet pebble,
Ribcage small as a child's fist
Arching under a drenched grey vest.
His underfeathers flattened and swirled by rain
Look like a map
Of the world's winds.

Pamela Gillilan

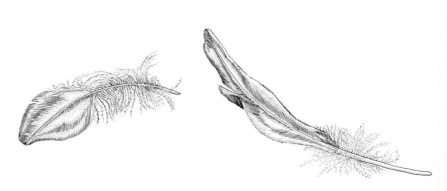

Airspace

Soviet airspace
American airspace
British airspace
it don't make sense to me
does it to you
said the eagle to the cuckoo
I always thought the air was free.

They're crazy
replied the cuckoo
plain crazy.
If the air belongs to anyone
it belongs to flying things
like me and you.
The air trusts our wings
and we trust the air.

That's true
that's true
said the eagle to the cuckoo.
But have no fear
I will spear the air
with wings for Korea bound.
The sky knows no limit.

Just a minute
just a minute
replied the cuckoo.
Didn't you hear
of the dove shot down to cinders
for flying too near the sea.
The airspace of the sea.

All airspace belongs to me
cried the eagle and away he flew.

I think I'll find a nest, said the cuckoo.

John Agard

Flying to Belfast, 1977

It was possible to laugh
as the engines whistled to the boil,

and wonder what the clouds looked like –
shovelled snow, Apple Charlotte,

Tufty Tails . . . I enjoyed
the Irish Sea, the ships were faults

in a dark expanse of linen.
And then Belfast below, a radio

with its back ripped off,
among the agricultural abstract

of the fields. Intricate,
neat and orderly. The windows

gleamed like drops of solder –
everything was wired up.

I thought of wedding presents,
white tea things

grouped on a dresser,
as we entered the cloud

and were nowhere –
a bride in a veil, laughing

at the sense of event, only
half afraid of an empty house

with its curtains boiling
from the bedroom window.

Craig Raine

Automatic Pilot Answers Back

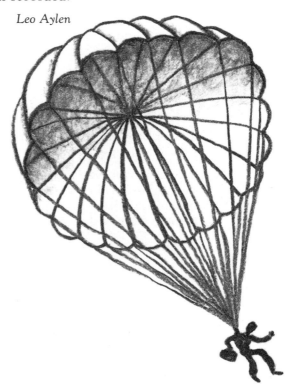

The pilot of Gulf Alpha Tango,
Cheesed to his teeth with delays –
Hours in a hold pattern
Circling that ten-mile radius from London airport,
Switched on the auto-pilot,
And, choosing his moment, parachuted out,
Landing neatly in his Battersea garden.
From there he phoned the control-tower:
'Gulf Alpha Tango is circling on auto-pilot.
It will run out of juice in twenty minutes.
Do something.'
The voice that replied
'Message received, understood,'
Was a tape he had himself recorded.

Leo Aylen

Your Machine

Sitting in the airport all alone
I felt I had to call you on the phone
I only got to talk to your machine
I tried to keep the message short and clean

I'm sure I must have sounded quite absurd
I know I didn't say the magic word
Time up I put the phone down with regret
I haven't learned to do it smoothly yet

To leave a message by machine
Is really quite an art
Your voice comes on and then the beep
And then it's time to start
It's hard to get the words out
Through the pounding of my heart

I never seem to say just what I mean
I'm tempted to be flippant or obscene
When panic trips my tongue I want to shout
Because I know that time is running out

I'm not so good at playing farewell scenes
And it makes me crazy
Talking to machines

Fran Landesman

The Tigers of Pain

The tigers of pain
Prowl out in the rain
Not far from the circle of light
Behind our locked doors
Their passionate roars
Assault us by day and by night

The famines and wars
On faraway shores
Send echoes that batter your heart
There's fire and flood
And spilling of blood
You wait for your troubles to start

When love comes along
Your head's full of song
It's hard to stay sober and sane
But be on your guard
For out in the yard
Are the terrible tigers of pain

Fran Landesman

The Fear

Fear came out of the forest
Fear walked under the sky
Fear breathed like death in his nostrils
And the wolf could not tell why.

He could not tell his brothers why
He could not tell them why
He who could read the torrent
And was cousin to the sky.

He who had howled with the west wind
And was brother to the rain
Who had suffered the fangs of the winter
And never told of his pain.

Who knew where danger lay lurking
Knew where the hunting was good
Knew each shaded water-hole
In each dark and secret wood.

He who was bravest of all the wolves
And feared nothing beneath the sky
Not the snake that struck from the deep green grass
Nor the eagle that clawed from the sky.

But even the bravest of all the wolves
The bravest beneath the sky
When he smelled the new fear in his nostrils
Could not tell his brothers why.

For the fear that walked out of the forest
The fear that crept over the snow
Was the age-old fear his fathers had known
A million years ago.

And the fear came walking on two legs
And in its hand was a bone
And the bone barked flames across the sky
And struck through his hide like a stone.

Better to have died on his mountain
Better to have died where he lay
Than to rot behind bars in a city
Making mankind a holiday.

Gareth Owen

Polar Bear

Hugging the wall, down
there in his open pit,
he ambles absently,
fitting his whole body
to the wide curve
of dingy cement.

Backwards and forwards
loping, big head weaving,
pressing one matted flank
and then the other
to the sun-scorched cliff
of his lonely prison.

His coat is far
from white – rather
a drab cream, with
yellow or brownish stains.
– He looks unhappy in the heat.
No wonder he never

turns to growl at
us, begging for attention.

James Kirkup

Giraffes

Earlier, licking the wood posts
Of their compound with grey
Slug tongues, or loping
In formation across the grass
Like a troupe of long-legged dancers,
The giraffes appeared so daft.

But now, as the rain begins,
And people rush for shelter
Like a crowd of panicked penguins,
The giraffes watch coolly
From their stately necks
With an air of condescension.

Vicki Feaver

Frost on the Shortest Day

A heavy frost last night,
The longest night of the year,
Makes the land at first light
Look spruced up for death,
Incurably white.

But the earth moving fast
Tips the shadow across
The field. It rolls past
Sheep who hold their ground
And into the hedge at last.

Not far behind, a track
Of frost is following
That the sun cannot lick
Completely green in time,
Before night rolls back.

Patricia Beer

Cold

Tonight the brittle trees
rattled and snapped in wind and the stars broke
trembling, like shattered ice.
Logs and frozen heather creaked
and starlight shook under our feet.

My son and I went onto the moor,
walking under drapes of a low sky.
A skull cracked underfoot;
a tarred roof winked; a snowball fell;
then quiet, that seemed to glow.
We came indoors when we had stared at snow.

Now we change our places at the hearth
like penguins on an ice floe. Draughts
enter through wall and roof: the swords
of cold sneak through our warmth
like poison threading liquid in a glass.

Glyn Hughes

One Gone, Eight to Go

On a night of savage frost,
This year, my smallest cat,
The fluffy one, got lost.
And I thought that that was that.

Until, late home, I heard,
As I fumbled for my key,
The weak sound of some bird.
He was there, mewing to me.

There, on the icy sill,
Lifting his crusted head,
He looked far worse than ill.
He looked, I'd say, quite dead.

Indoors, though, he could eat,
And he showed, and fluffed his tail.
So much for a plate of meat.
So much for a storm of hail.

Now, by the burning grate,
I stroke his fragile spine,
Thinking of time, and fate.
Lives go. Men don't have nine,

As kittens do, to waste.
This lucky one survives,
And purrs, affronted-faced.
But even he, who thrives

Tonight, in my cupped hands,
And will grow big and grey,
Will sense, in time, the sands,
And fail, and shrink away.

George Macbeth

Cat Camouflage

In winter the trees do not move.
Half the lawn is coppered with leaves,
Scollops under the bare trees.

There is no sky
Only a snow-blue sheet behind.
A ginger cat goes from copper into green:
I do not know when it reaches bushes
To stalk unwary birds;
Its form blends with the world's
As one season strays into another
While all else stays the same.

Alan Sillitoe

Night

The new moon's bowl
Pours out its liquid light.
All colour gone
The scene is starkly bright,
Deep wells of darkness
Shallow pools of light.
While from an upstairs window
A frost-bleached field
Is a lake that floods
Far out into the weald.
The road's river glistens
On which the vehicles ride,
And flakey moths
Are bobbing on the tide
Of air. The white-rigged owl,
Which drifts from barn to tree,
Ghost-ships it on the airy sea.
Meanwhile the wary mouse
Finds its safe harbour
In a nearby house.
The world is theirs
During these moonlit hours,
Until the dawn breaks
And once more it's ours.

John Cotton

Winter Dawn

Dawn and only the snow penetrates the silence
Falling like footsteps with a guilty secret.
This is a still world stripped of action,
A dark white world of perpetual waiting.

The thick snow becomes a coat of many colours
As a mauve light creeps in from the east.

As the world wakes up a deer clears a wire fence
Haunted by the habit of being hunted.

Alan Bold

Morning

The white egg boils in the new saucepan
The toaster flips another toast upwards.
The window is open on the drenched field
where the calf is loose again among the haystacks.

Our jobs await us but the radio says
'Love is everything.' The disc jockey
is brushed and frivolous beside the mike
speaking of streets and towns he hasn't seen.

The road points the house towards the office.
The hens are laying eggs. Someone bakes bread.
We hammer the calf's stake into the ground
Around the iron fades the fresh dew.

Iain Crichton Smith

Tractor

The tractor stands frozen – an agony
To think of. All night
Snow packed its open entrails. Now a head-pincering gale,
A spill of molten ice, smoking snow,
Pours into its steel.
At white heat of numbness it stands
In the aimed hosing of ground-level fieriness.

It defies flesh and won't start.
Hands are like wounds already
Inside armour gloves, and feet are unbelievable
As if the toe-nails were all just torn off.
I stare at it in hatred. Beyond it
The copse hisses – capitulates miserably
In the fleeing, failing light. Starlings,
A dirtier sleetier snow, blow smokily, unendingly, over
Towards plantations Eastward.
All the time the tractor is sinking
Through the degrees, deepening
Into its hell of ice.

The starting lever
Cracks its action, like a snapping knuckle.
The battery is alive – but like a lamb
Trying to nudge its solid-frozen mother –
While the seat claims my buttock-bones, bites
With the space-cold of earth, which it has joined
In one solid lump.

I squirt commercial sure-fire
Down the black throat – it just coughs.
It ridicules me – a trap of iron stupidity
I've stepped into. I drive the battery
As if I were hammering and hammering
The frozen arrangement to pieces with a hammer
And it jabbers laughing pain-crying mockingly
Into happy life.

And stands
Shuddering itself full of heat, seeming to enlarge slowly
Like a demon demonstrating
A more-than-usually-complete materialisation –
Suddenly it jerks from its solidarity
With the concrete, and lurches towards a stanchion
Bursting with superhuman well-being and abandon
Shouting Where Where?

Worse iron is waiting. Power-lift kneels,
Levers awake imprisoned deadweight,
Shackle-pins bedded in cast-iron cow-shit.
The blind and vibrating condemned obedience
Of iron to the cruelty of iron,
Wheels screeched out of their night-locks –

Fingers
Among the tormented
Tonnage and burning of iron

Eyes
Weeping in the wind of chloroform

And the tractor, streaming with sweat,
Raging and trembling and rejoicing.

Ted Hughes

Interference

bringing you live
the final preparations
for this great mission
should be coasting
the rings of Saturn
two years time
cloudless sky, and
an unparalleled
world coverage
we have countdown

ten
may not have told you
   nine
the captain's mascot
   eight
miniaturized gonk
   seven
chief navigator
   six
had twins Tuesday
   five
the Eiffel Tower for
   four
comparison, gantries
   three
aside, so the fuel
   two
huge cloud of
   one
a perfect
   a half
I don't quite
   a quarter
something has clearly
   an eighth
we do not have lift-off
   a sixteenth
we do not have lift-off
   a thirty-second
we do not have lift-off
   a sixty-fourth
we do not have lift-off
   a hundred and twenty-eighth
wo de nat hove loft-iff

     Edwin Morgan

Martians

Hey, Brother Soul,
suppose
you woke up,
one morning,
and heard, on the radio,
that the Martians had landed,
and they were Black
but were a little bit rough
on the other brothers on earth,
because they're white,
would you go out to meet them
on a mission of arbitration?

Rudolph Kizerman

Transplant

Wat a ting eena news, mi dear ma!
Whole heap o' tings a gwan,
Man a dead, an' steel a strike
An' twenty-six week baby a bawn.

But de ting wha sweet mi in de news
An' cause mi fi start tek t'ought,
Is de wey docta a play 'pass de ball'
Wid nedda people heart.

Newspaper say dat t'irteen smaddy
Get heart transplant a'ready.
An' it look like de nex' one on de lis'
Is Katie bad dawg, Freddie.

Kate sey if docta can a change
Man heart, liva, an' kidney,
It shouldn' be hard fi change de heart
O' one li' deggey puppy.

She sey Freddie dis a bite up people,
An' dah play tug-o-war wid dem foot.
An councillor ben t'reaten fi put im dung,
Wen im nyam up im wife boot.

She cyan tek chance tek out im teet',
For den im couldn' eat, fi a start,
So she decide bes' ting fi do,
Is fi tek out im bad-mine heart.

So she a cyah im go dung a de vet
Mek im see wha im cyan do,
For she wooden mine change im bull-dog heart,
Fi one nice, likkle, sweet poodle.

But puttin fun an joke aside,
Is a big step wi dis tek.
John sey no too long from dis wi wi' start
Transplant hand an' foot an' nek.

An' fi im wife, Lizzy, chat so much,
All im bizniz she let i' out.
It wooda please im heart fi si
Smaddy transplant har mout'.

Valerie Bloom

War Movie Veteran

You can't tell me a thing that I don't know
About combat, son. I reckon I've seen them all
On the big screen or TV, the late-night show
Or Sunday matinee. I'm what you'd call
An old campaigner; some of them I've seen
Four, five times maybe. I've got so's I
Can tell for sure which ones among that green
Platoon of rookies are the guys to die.
You know the sensitive and quiet kid
Who can't stand rough-stuff, says his prayers at night
And never cusses? He's got to wind up dead
But not before we've seen that he can fight
And he's got guts. He ain't afraid to kill
Once the chips are down. The one to see
Turn really yellow is the loud-mouthed mother
That talks like he ain't scared of nothing, he
Will go, expendable. So will the other,
The black guy who's as good as you or me,
And the Jew that's seeking vengeance for his brother.
The comedian – the hero's buddy – could
Come through the battle in one piece or not:
He's only there for laughs, that's understood
By veterans like me. The hero's got
To be alive and kicking at the end.
The one I really like – you know the guy –
The tough top-sergeant, nobody's best friend,
His favourite meal is bullets, blood and rye;
The Krauts he's killed is anybody's guess.
He's made of steel and leather, but you'll find
That he can be the soul of gentleness
With scared old ladies, babies and the blind
Pooch whose master's been knocked off. But never
Think the guy's gone soft: back under fire
He's just as cold and murderous as ever,
He's everything a General could desire.
He'll come through safe okay.

                    I tell you, son.
I could write out the list of casualties
Long before the battle has begun.
I've seen it all. I know the way it is
And got to be. Well, that's what you could call
The human side, psychology I guess.
The other stuff – a cinch to learn it all
In half a dozen battles, maybe less.
It takes no time to get the different ranks:
Enlisted men and noncoms, officers,
The names of hardware, ammunition, tanks
And how the thing is planned. You'll think at first
That war is chaos, howl of bullet, shell
And bomb; flashes and thunder as they burst,
Flying shit, hot jig-saw bits of hell.
Not so. It's all worked out before the start.
It's choreographed, like in a dance, okay?
You get to know the pattern. War's an art,
It's one I understand. There ain't no way
That you'll find anyone to tell you more
Than me about realities of war.

                    Vernon Scannell

Military Service

He will not hurt because he is afraid.
He tries to force a hate he does not feel.
He practises all night but is dismayed
When morning comes to shine upon his steel
To find he handles it as if he played

With caps and pistols, noise which never hurt.
He has a bayonet and feels the knife
With fingering pride. He has become alert
As if to kill would give him double life
But plunging steel in sawdust dulls his heart.

He has not proved his manhood, thinks of waste,
Of sweating hours when he's too bored to read.
Then anger starts that he has been so placed,
Playing the guard of other's fear and greed.
His fight is like loveless kisses, a sour taste.

Elizabeth Jennings

There's a War On

'Don't you know
There's a war on?'
They used to say
Forty years ago,
Whenever we threw away
Waste paper we should have saved, or dropped
Two lumps of sugar in our tea,
Or, from an undrawn blind,
Let a windowful of light
Beam out into the night –
'There's a war on!
Has nobody told you?'

No war now.
Clouds
Float calmly over
Barricades in the street, feet
Crashing on broken glass, crowds
Setting fire to cars,
Bombs in the Market Square;
Girls, old men, soldiers, faces hot
With anger, presidents shot;
A child sobbing in the cold night air –
There's a peace on!
Has nobody told them?

Norman Nicholson

Angel Hill

A sailor came walking down Angel Hill,
He knocked on my door with a right good will,
With a right good will he knocked on my door.
He said, 'My friend, we have met before.'
  No, never, said I.

He searched my eye with a sea-blue stare
And he laughed aloud on the Cornish air,
On the Cornish air he laughed aloud
And he said, 'My friend, you have grown too proud.'
  No, never, said I.

'In war we swallowed the bitter bread
And drank of the brine,' the sailor said.
'We took of the bread and we tasted the brine
As I bound your wounds and you bound mine.'
  No, never, said I.

'By day and night on the diving sea
We whistled to sun and moon,' said he.
'Together we whistled to moon and sun
And vowed our stars should be as one.'
  No, never, said I.

'And now,' he said, 'that the war is past
I come to your hearth and home at last.
I come to your home and hearth to share
Whatever fortune waits me there.'
  No, never, said I.

'I have no wife nor son,' he said,
'Nor pillow on which to lay my head,
No pillow have I, nor wife nor son,
Till you shall give to me my own.'
  No, never, said I.

His eye it flashed like a lightning-dart
And still as a stone then stood my heart.
My heart as a granite stone was still
And he said, 'My friend, but I think you will.'
  No, never, said I.

The sailor smiled and turned in his track
And shifted the bundle on his back
And I heard him sing as he strolled away,
'You'll send and you'll fetch me one fine day.'
  No, never, said I.

Charles Causley

Not Better – Just Not As Bad
A Fable

The animals one day were having a debate
about the problems of contemporary war
and nuclear arms. The deer said: 'I hate
those senseless weapons of mass destruction
that can wipe out entire herds, and more –
the whole forest, perhaps, in one blind eruption.'

'How I agree with you!' replied the mouse.
'In the old days, at least one was fairly well
protected from explosions in one's own snug house.'
'Yes, that is so,' agreed the hippopotamus. 'In the First
World War, an animal was hit by shrapnell or by shell
but very rarely – a slight cut at the worst.'

The panther nodded sagely. 'But in World War Two
things became much worse, as I recall.
There was danger in the streets, and even in the Zoo.
Not only we animals, but women, children, trees and flowers
were exposed to death or mutilation when the bombs would fall
on some defenceless street or park for hours and hours.'

Then the ancient elephant spoke up: 'I well recall,'
he quietly declared, 'those days you think were better, kinder
than today. But in that distant time, there were already all
kinds of weapons – bows, arrows, slings and traps they had:
and men were just as cruel, greedy, thoughtless – even blinder
than now. The world was then no better – just not as bad.'

James Kirkup

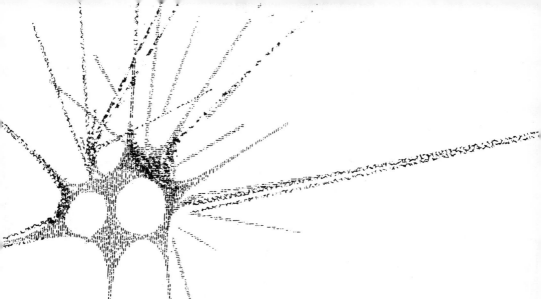

That Star

That star
Will blow your hand off
That star
Will scramble your brains and your nerves
That star
Will frazzle your skin off
That star
Will turn everybody yellow and stinking
That star
Will scorch everything dead fumed to its blueprint
That star
Will make the earth melt
That star ... and so on.

And they surround us. And far into infinity.
These are the armies of the night.
There is no escape.
Not one of them is good, or friendly, or corruptible.

One chance remains: KEEP ON DIGGING THAT HOLE

KEEP ON DIGGING AWAY AT THAT HOLE

Ted Hughes

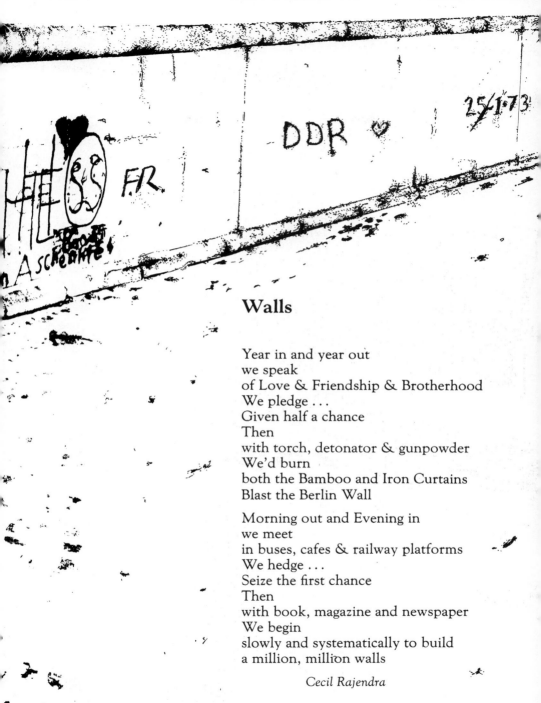

Walls

Year in and year out
we speak
of Love & Friendship & Brotherhood
We pledge ...
Given half a chance
Then
with torch, detonator & gunpowder
We'd burn
both the Bamboo and Iron Curtains
Blast the Berlin Wall

Morning out and Evening in
we meet
in buses, cafes & railway platforms
We hedge ...
Seize the first chance
Then
with book, magazine and newspaper
We begin
slowly and systematically to build
a million, million walls

Cecil Rajendra

Adman

I'm the new man
in the ivory tower
the new man
the man with the power
the old village chief
used to lay down the law
but the medicine man
had his foot in the door
he taught me the secret
of how you tick
to use psychology
like a conjuring trick
so I've found the doorway
into your brain
when you get a bargain
you lose – I gain
I can get in your bath
I can get in your bed
I can get in your pants
I can get in your head
you're like a man on the cross
you're like a priest at the stake
you're like a fish on a hook
make no mistake
I can tie you up
I can take you down
I can sit and watch
you wriggle around
'cos I'm the medicine man
with the media touch
the man with the power that's
too much

Nigel Gray

Mad Ad

A Madison Avenue whizzkid
thought it a disgrace
That no one had exploited
the possibilities in space
Discussed it with a client
who agreed and very soon
A thousand miles of neontubing
were transported to the moon.

Now no one can ignore it
the product's selling fine
The night they turned the moon
into a Coca-Cola sign.

Roger McGough

Heavenly Vaults

Where banks all look like temples,
　And temples look like banks,
Where does one count his blessings?
　Where does one offer thanks?

You sense the holy places
　By the faces in the ranks,
The bankrupt in the temples,
　The worshipful in banks.

E. Y. Harburg

Where Have all the Wise Men Gone?

Where have all the wise men gone?
Following which star?
Carrying which costly gifts
From a supermart bazaar?

Are they looking for the same child
Sought two thousand years ago
Across that eastern desert
Our dreams have turned to snow?

Will they know when they have found him
When they've travelled long and hard?
Will they try to pay his manger bill
With a plastic credit card?

And if it is the same child
Peace halo-promised round his brow,
Will today's dark-suited wise men
Understand his message now?

John Kitching

The Centre

We look straight up through the trees
And suspect the sky is there, above us,
Patiently waiting to bless our days.

But no – we are underneath the sky,
It tolerates us with gravity,
Its blue obliterates the egocentric I.

Beyond that we feel space to be out there
Instead of acknowledging year after year
We monotonously hang around one star.

If our sunny star suddenly went out,
If space was deprived of all human thought,
If there was one less light in an inhuman night –

Nothing would alter in the eternity of space,
There would simply be one star less,
That vastness would not care about us.

We are at the centre of nothing
Like prisoners forced around in a ring
Because someone somewhere has done something wrong.

Alan Bold

How's That?

How's that?
Asks the bowler –
Pad before wicket,
Feet splayed awry, wrist higher
Than shoulder, a comic cartoon of cricket –
Not out,
Says the Umpire.

How's that?
Ask the Neighbours –
Sacked from his job with the Dole Queue for a hobby,
Cheques bounced by the Bank, wife
Run off with the lodger, bailiff's in the lobby –
Not out,
Says Life.

How's that?
Asks the Justice –
Nabbed red-handed, stranded with no hope,
And a hundred willing hands ready to shove
A branded man still lower down the slope –
Not out,
Says Love.

How's that?
Asks the Doctor –
Four score years and ten,
With a gurgle in the bronchials, a growling in the breath,
Appealing for a re-play, life over once again –
Out,
Says Death.

Norman Nicholson

Days

They come to us
Empty but not clean
Like unrinsed bottles

Sides clouded
With a film
Of yesterday.

We can't keep them
Except in diaries
And photographs:

Our task
Is to fill up
And return.

There are no wages.
The reward is said to be
The work itself.

And if we question this –
Get angry, scream
At their round clock faces

Or try to break the glass –
We only hurt ourselves,
The days remain intact.

Days are indestructible.
Even night
With dark and sleep

Is not their weakness
But a tease
To make us dream of death.

There is no end to days –
Only a cloth laid
Over a birdcage.

Vicki Feaver

Days

What are days for?
Days are where we live.
They come, they wake us
Time and time over.
They are to be happy in:
Where can we live but days?

Ah, solving that question
Brings the priest and the doctor
In their long coats
Running over the fields.

Philip Larkin

Children's Questions

Julian (aged 4)

We follow down the turning stair
Into a room far underground,
Regard the scratched stone walls, sense fear
And horror grained on every inch.
'If you will keep your children near,
I'll put the light out, so you'll see
How dark it was.' A switch somewhere
Imprisons us. The dungeon's dark
Is absolute. Silenced, we hear
The nothing prisoners heard, watch for
The glimmering that should appear
When eyes have grown accustomed. Close,
A child whispers, 'Are we still here?'

Maria (aged 10)

'How do we know,' the child asked, 'that
We're not dreaming all this?' – meaning
The world, our whole experience.
Ten years of living shaped the thought;
Ten more have hidden what I said.
Perhaps it was, 'The dream seems real.'
'Perhaps our dreams are real,' she said.

John Loveday

Index of Titles and First Lines

Acknowledgements

The poems in this book are reproduced by kind permission of the copyright holders as indicated below.

John Agard: 'Hairstyle', 'Airspace' and 'On the disco floor', all © John Agard. Reprinted by permission of the author. **Leo Aylen:** 'Automatic Pilot Answers Back' © 1986 Leo Aylen. Reprinted by permission of the author. **Patricia Beer:** 'Frost on the Shortest Day'. Reprinted by permission of the author. **James Berry:** 'Kept Home', © 1986 James Berry. Reprinted by permission of the author. **Valerie Bloom:** 'Transplant' from *Touch Mi! Tell Mi!*. Reprinted by permission of Bogle-L'Ouverture Publications Ltd. **Alan Bold:** 'The Swimmer', 'The Centre' and 'Winter Dawn'. All reprinted by permission of the author. **Keith Bosley:** 'Snapshots', 'Dog Exercising Man' and 'The Silence Lesson', all © 1986 Keith Bosley. Reprinted by permission of the author. **Edward Kamau Brathwaite:** 'Slow Guitar' from *Rights of Passage*, © OUP 1965. Reprinted by permission of Oxford University Press. **Alan Brownjohn:** 'You'll See' from *Collected Poems 1952–83*. Reprinted by permission of Secker & Warburg Limited. **Charles Causley:** 'Angel Hill' from *Collected Poems* (Macmillan). Reprinted by permission of David Higham Associates Limited. **Faustin Charles:** 'Viv'. Reprinted by permission of the author. **Stanley Cook:** 'The Long Walk' and 'Beginner's Luck', both © 1986 Stanley Cook. Reprinted by permission of the author. **John Cotton:** 'Night', © 1986 John Cotton. Reprinted by permission of the author. **Vicki Feaver:** 'Giraffes' and 'Days' from *Close Relatives*. Reprinted by permission of Secker & Warburg Ltd. **Tony Flynn:** 'Boats for Hire' from *A Rumoured City* (ed. Douglas Dunn). Reprinted by permission of the author and Bloodaxe Books Limited. **Pamela Gillilan:** 'Kestrel'. First published in *Anglo Welsh Review*, Issue #70, 1982. Reprinted by permission of the author. **Mick Gowar:** 'Hero' from *So Far, So Good*, © Mick Gowar 1986. Reprinted by permission of Collins Publishers and Murray Pollinger; 'Christmas Thank You's' from *Swings and Roundabouts*, © Mick Gowar 1981. Reprinted by permission of Collins Publishers. **Nigel Gray:** 'Adman', © 1986 Nigel Gray. Reprinted by permission of the author. **Andrew Hall:** 'Whippet' from *Iron Age Anthology* (Iron Press). Reprinted by permission of the author. **E Y Harburg:** 'Heavenly Vaults' from *At This Point In Rhyme*, copyright © 1976 by E Y Harburg. Reprinted by permission of Crown Publishers, Inc., USA. **Gregory Harrison:** 'The Perch Pool', © 1986 Gregory Harrison. Reprinted by permission of the author. **Seamus Heaney:** 'Mother Of The Groom' and 'Good Night' from *Wintering Out* (Faber and Faber Ltd); 'The Salmon Fisher to the Salmon' from *Door Into the Dark* (Faber). These poems are published in the US in *Poems 1965–1975* (Farrar Strauss & Giroux, Inc), Copyright © 1966, 1969, 1972, 1975, 1980 by Seamus Heaney and are reprinted by permission of the publishers. **Phoebe Hesketh:** 'Heatwave' and 'Kingfisher' from *A Song of Sunlight* originally published by Chatto & Windus, and reproduced by permission of The Bodley Head. **Geoffrey Holloway:** 'Cinquains', © 1986 Geoffrey Holloway. Reprinted by permission of the author. **Glyn Hughes:** 'Cold'. First published in *Best of Neighbours* (Ceolfrith Press). Reprinted by permission of the author and the Northern Centre for Contemporary Art. **Ted Hughes:** 'Foxhunt', 'Tractor' and 'That Star' (Stanza 4 of 'Four Tales Told by An Idiot') from *Moortown*, copyright © 1979 by Ted Hughes. Reprinted by permission of Faber & Faber Ltd, and Harper & Row, Publishers, Inc. **Elizabeth Jennings:** 'Absence' from *A Sense of the World* (Deutsch) and 'Military Service' from *Consequently I Rejoice*. Reprinted by permission of David Higham Associates Limited. **Erica Jong:** 'There is Only One Story' from *Ordinary Miracles* (Plume, NAL). Copyright © 1983 Erica Mann Jong. Reprinted by permission of The Sterling Lord Agency, Inc. **Richard Kell:** 'Pigeons' from *Differences*. Reprinted by permission of Chatto & Windus for the author. **James Kirkup:** 'One Way of Flying', 'Gymnast', 'Polar Bear', and 'Not better – Just Not As Bad', all © 1986 James Kirkup. Reprinted by permission of the author. **John Kitching:** 'Where Have All the Wise Men Gone?', © 1986 John Kitching. Reprinted by permission of the author. **Fran Landesman:** 'Your Machine', 'The Tigers of Pain' and 'You Make Me So Nervous' from *Is It Overcrowded In Heaven?* All reprinted by permission of Jay Landesman. **Philip Larkin:** 'Days' from *The Whitsun Weddings*. Reprinted by permission of Faber & Faber Limited. **Brian Lee:** 'Going', © 1986 Brian Lee. Reprinted by permission of the author. **Laurie Lee:** 'Town Owl', from *Selected Poems* (1983). Reprinted by permission of André Deutsch. **Maurice Lindsay:** 'Attending a Football Match' from *Collected Poems*, published by Paul Harris, Edinburgh. Reprinted with permission. **Liz Lochhead:** 'Riddle-Me-Ree' from *Dreaming Frankenstein and Collected Poems*. Reprinted by permission of Polygon Books. **John Loveday:** 'Children's Questions'. Used by permission of the author. **Liz Loxley:** 'The Thickness of Ice' from *Hard Lines: New Poetry and Prose*. Reprinted by permission of Faber & Faber Ltd. **George MacBeth:** 'Rain', in *The Language Book* (ILEA English Centre). Reprinted by permission of Anthony Sheil Associates Ltd., Literary Agents: 'One Gone, Eight to Go' from *Poems From Oby*, Copyright © 1982 George MacBeth. Reprinted by permission of Secker & Warburg Limited and Atheneum Publishers, Inc. **Roger McGough:** 'The

Unincredible Hulk-in-Law', 'Beatings' and 'Cup Final' from *Sky In The Pie* (Kestrel Books); 'Mad Ad' from *In The Glassroom* (Jonathan Cape Ltd); 'Hundreds and Thousands' from *Hundreds and Thousands* (Puffin Books). All reprinted by permission of A D Peters & Co Ltd. **Ian McMillan:** 'Can't be bothered to think of a title', © 1986 Ian McMillan. Reprinted by permission of the author. **Wes Magee:** 'Growing Up' and 'Elvis – the poem' both © 1986 Wes Magee. Reprinted by permission of the author. **Adrian Mitchell:** 'Lost Love Poem' and 'The Fox' both © 1984 by Adrian Mitchell, first published in *Nothingmas Day* by Allison & Busby. Used with permission. 'Watch Your Step – I'm Drenched' from *The Apeman Cometh*. Reprinted by permission of Jonathan Cape Ltd, for the author. **Edwin Morgan:** 'Interference' from *From Glasgow to Saturn* (Carcanet). Reprinted by permission of the author. **Judith Nicholls:** 'Transformations' © 1986 Judith Nicholls. Reprinted by permission of the author. **Norman Nicholson:** 'There's a War On' and 'How's That?', both © 1986 Norman Nicholson. Reprinted by permission of the author. **Leslie Norris:** 'A Girl's Song' from *Ransoms*. Reprinted by permission of Chatto & Windus for the author. **Philip Oakes:** 'Live Baiting' from *Selected Poems* (André Deutsch Ltd). Copyright © 1982 by Philip Oakes. Reprinted by permission of Elaine Green Ltd. **Gareth Owen:** 'Street Boy' and 'The Fear'. Reprinted by permission of the author. **Brian Patten:** 'Sometimes it Happens' from *Love Poems*. Reprinted by permission of George Allen & Unwin (Publishing) Ltd. **Gordon Phillips:** 'Guitarman', © 1986 Gordon Phillips. Reprinted by permission of the author. **Patricia Pogson:** 'Earrings', © 1986 Patricia Pogson. Reprinted by permission of the author. **Craig Raine:** 'Flying to Belfast, 1977' from *A Martian Sends a Postcard Home*, © Craig Raine 1979. Reprinted by permission of Oxford University Press. **Cecil Rajendra:** 'Walls' from *Bones and Feathers*. Reprinted by permission of Heinemann (Malaysia) Sdn Bhd. **Michael Rosen:** 'I'm the Big Sleeper' from *Mind Your Own Business*. Reprinted by permission of André Deutsch. **Vernon Scannell:** 'War Movie Veteran', © 1986 Vernon Scannell. Reprinted by permission of the author. **Ian Serraillier:** 'The Film Star', © 1977 Ian Serraillier, from *The Sun Goes Free* (Longman Group Ltd). Reprinted by permission of the author. **Alan Sillitoe:** 'Cat Camouflage, © 1986 Alan Sillitoe. Reprinted by permission of the author. **Iain Crichton Smith:** 'Morning' from *Selected Poems*. Reprinted by permission of Macdonald Publishers. **Kit Wright:** 'Hundreds and Thousands' from *Hot Dog and Other Poems* (Kestrel Books, 1981), copyright © 1981 by Kit Wright, pp.62–63. Reprinted by permission of Penguin Books Ltd.

Every effort has been made to contact copyright owners but sometimes without success. The publisher will rectify any errors or omissions in future editions if notified.

The publishers would like to thank the following for permission to reproduce photographs:

David Agar pp.50–51; Barnaby's Picture Library pp.44–45, 108–109; Janet and Colin Bord pp.90–91; Patrick Eagar p.60; Richard and Sally Greenhill pp.8, 8–9 (bottom left), 9 (top left), 78, 84–85; Rob Judges pp.18–19; Frank Lane pp.68–69; Marshalls (Photographers) of Camberley pp.98–99; Network pp.16, 58–59, 81, 104–105; Rosie Potter pp.9 (top right), 12–13; Retna Pictures pp. 24–25; Rex Features pp.92–93; Royal Naval Museum, Portsmouth pp.100–101; Sporting Pictures pp.56–57; Syndication International p.23; Jeff Tabberner pp.32–33; Topham Picture Library pp.40–41, 83.

The illustrations are by Mike Atkinson, Laura Boyd, Sue Heap, Gerard Gibson, Kathleen Lindsley, Vanessa Luff, Alan Marks, Amelia Rosato, Nick Sharratt, Linda Smith, Freire Wright.